Taking Shape

From GRAIN to BREAD

NICOLA BAXTER

SIMON & SCHUSTER
YOUNG BOOKS

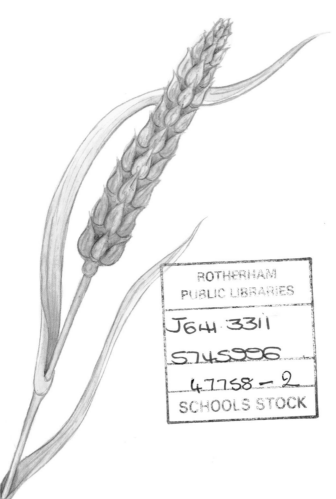

Acknowledgements

The author and publishers would like to thank the following for their assistance: Lynette Baxter, The National Association of Master Bakers, The Flour Advisory Bureau and Mono Equipment Ltd.

First published in 1993
by Simon & Schuster Young Books

© 1993 Simon & Schuster Young Books
Simon & Schuster Young Books,
Campus 400, Maylands Avenue,
Hemel Hempstead, Herts HP2 7EZ.

Designer: Janet Watson
Illustrator: Katy Sleight
Commissioning editor: Debbie Fox

Printed in Portugal by Edições ASA

A CIP catalogue record for this book is available from the British Library.

ISBN 0 7500 1318 4

Contents

All sorts of bread

For thousands of years, the seeds of specially grown grasses, called grains, have been the main food for most human beings. Grains include wheat, barley, rye, oats, maize and rice. Which kind of grain is eaten depends on the climate and growing conditions of each country.

A convenient way to eat grain is to make it into loaves, rolls or biscuits. The examples shown here are all made by mixing ground-up grain with other ingredients and shaping and baking it. How many sorts have you eaten?

But before bread can be made, the grain has to be planted, grown and harvested.

Growing grain

Today most bread is made from wheat. Wheat grows best in places that have rich soil, warm summers, cool winters and some but not too much rain. Large areas of grassland, such as the prairies of the United States or the steppes of Russia, have been ploughed to grow grain crops, known as cereals.

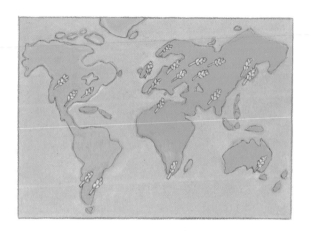

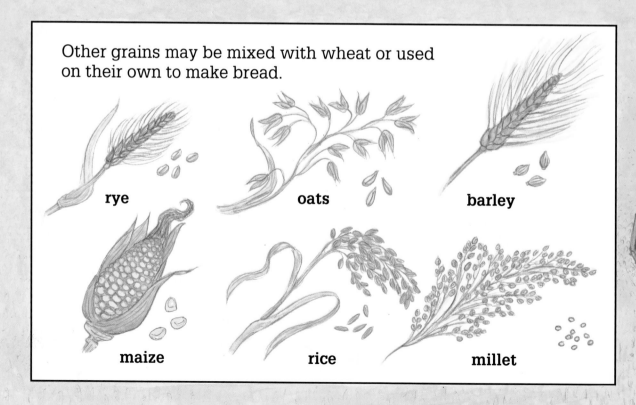

Other grains may be mixed with wheat or used on their own to make bread.

rye

oats

barley

maize

rice

millet

As it ripens, the green wheat turns a golden brown. It is the seed head of the wheat that is harvested to be ground into flour. Scientists work to develop wheat that is suitable for different growing conditions around the world. The stalks and leaves are cut for straw.

The seed head or ear holds each grain in a covering called a husk.

The stem has to be strong enough to support the grains and not be flattened by wind or rain.

The small green leaves of young wheat convert energy from the sun to feed the plant.

A combine harvester is used to cut the ripe grain. The grain may need to be dried with hot air before it can be stored.

Large lorries take the wheat to be dried in huge grain stores or straight to the mill.

After harvesting, ploughing the stubble into the soil instead of burning it is thought to help the environment.

From grain to flour

Grinding grain into flour is called milling.
First the grain passes through machines
that clean it to remove dirt, husks and any
rubbish. The flour may be wholemeal flour,
using all the grain, or white flour that uses
only the starchy centre of the seed.

Water may be added
to soften the outer
layer and make the
starchy middle easy
to release.

One kind of wheat may
be mixed with other
kinds of wheat to give
the flour different
properties. This is
called gristing.

The grain then
passes through a
series of rollers
and sieves.

Break rollers split the
grain to release the
starchy white middle
called the endosperm.

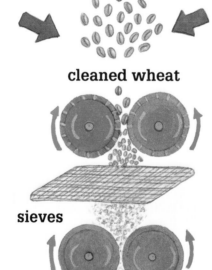

cleaned wheat

sieves

reducing
rollers

sieves

Reducing rollers crush
the endosperm
particles ("semolina")
into white flour.

For wholemeal flour,
bran and wheatgerm
are mixed.

Bran and wheatgerm
are used in breakfast
cereals, animal feed or
sold as health food.

Each grain of wheat would grow into a new wheat plant if it was left to fall to the ground. There are three main parts to the grain. The germ sprouts to grow into the new plant. The starchy white endosperm provides food for the new young plant before it can take food from the soil. The outer case or bran protects the young seed.

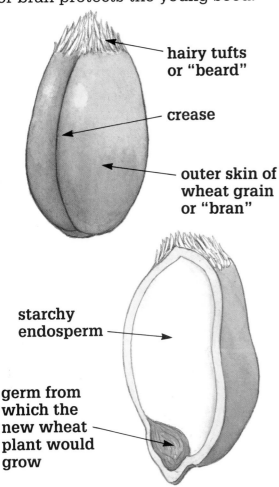

hairy tufts or "beard"

crease

outer skin of wheat grain or "bran"

starchy endosperm

germ from which the new wheat plant would grow

This picture of the inside of a grain of wheat is much bigger than in real life.

It is really this size:

Try this!

1 Spread some wholemeal flour on coloured paper and look at it carefully. What different kinds of particles can you see?

2 Take another piece of coloured paper and carefully shake some of the wholemeal flour on to it through a fine sieve. What kind of flour do you see on the paper? What is left in the sieve?

Many foods contain flour. Look at the labels on food packaging to find some that do. Why do you think flour is used in these foods?

13

From flour to dough

Bread can be made by hand in a small kitchen, one loaf at a time, or it can be made in huge bakeries where everything is done by machine, and thousands of loaves are made at the same time. Whichever way it is made, the main stages are the same.

wheat flour, sometimes mixed with extra bran or other grains

yeast to make the bread rise and be light and spongy

Most bread is made from a mixture of these ingredients.

improvers, often including ascorbic acid (vitamin C), which helps the yeast to work more quickly

vegetable fat to make the bread lighter and keep fresh for longer

water

salt to improve the flavour

Bread dough is very gluey and sticky. This is because flour contains a protein called gluten that mixes with water. Dough made from flour with a lot of gluten can stretch well to trap the air that makes the bread light and spongy. This kind of flour is called strong flour.

In large bakeries a computer controls how much of each ingredient is used.

14

Bread for health

Bread contains lots of the kinds of foods that our bodies need. Have a look at a bread wrapping to see how much of these foods the bread contains.

A wholemeal loaf contains:

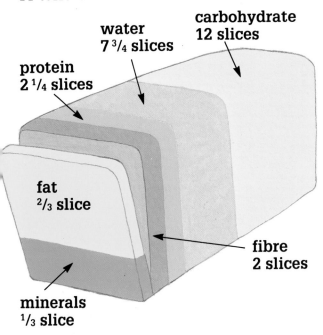

water
7 ³/₄ slices

carbohydrate
12 slices

protein
2 ¹/₄ slices

fat
²/₃ slice

fibre
2 slices

minerals
¹/₃ slice

carbohydrate – for energy

protein – to help bones and muscles grow and repair themselves

fibre – to help food move quickly through our bodies and be properly digested. Wheat bran is a kind of fibre.

group B vitamins – for good health, nerves and digestion

minerals – such as iron for healthy blood and calcium for strong bones and teeth

Try this!

You can compare the amount of gluten in strong flour and ordinary plain flour.

1 In a small mixing bowl, mix together 25 g of strong bread flour with enough water to make a small ball of dough.

2 Try stretching the dough to see how elastic it is. Then make a ball again.

3 Hold the dough under a cold tap. Squeeze it gently until the water runs clear. The cloudy water contained the starch has washed out of the dough. In your hand is the gluten.

4 Now try with ordinary plain flour. What happens?

Shaping and proving

Bread can be flat and crispy, or light and spongy. Light bread has lots of air trapped in it, and yeast is used to make this happen.

In a bakery, bread is usually allowed to rise, or "prove", twice. The first time is after the dough is mixed. By adding improvers to the dough and mixing vigorously, this proving happens quite fast. The bubbles from the yeast make the dough double in size.

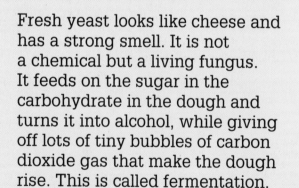

Fresh yeast looks like cheese and has a strong smell. It is not a chemical but a living fungus. It feeds on the sugar in the carbohydrate in the dough and turns it into alcohol, while giving off lots of tiny bubbles of carbon dioxide gas that make the dough rise. This is called fermentation.

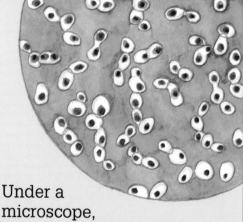

Under a microscope, you can see yeast cells dividing. This is called budding. A new cell grows and then separates from its parent cell.

Yeast needs the right conditions to make bubbles of gas. Try some tests to find out what these are.

You will need:
3 small plastic bottles
sugar
warm and cold water
fresh yeast
3 stretched balloons
a teaspoon (tsp)

1 Mark the bottles and fill them:

A – ½ full warm water, 1 tsp sugar, ½ tsp yeast
B – ½ full warm water, ½ tsp yeast
C – ½ full cold water, 1 tsp sugar, ½ tsp yeast

2 Swirl the bottles to mix the contents. Don't shake too much.

3 Tie a balloon on the top of each bottle.

4 Put A and B in a warm place and C in a cold place. Have a look from time to time during the day. What happens?

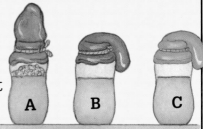

Then the dough is kneaded by a machine and divided into pieces of the right size for the type of bread being made. These may be dropped into tins to make loaves, or arranged on trays to make rolls. The tins for sandwich loaves have lids on them so that the tops of the loaves stay flat.

After this the dough is left to prove again for about 50 minutes until it has almost doubled in size. It is then ready for baking.

From dough to bread

In a large bakery, the proved loaves and rolls pass through huge ovens on a conveyor belt. They move slowly through the oven for about 20 minutes. When they come out the other side they are perfectly cooked. Along the side of the oven there are windows so that the bakers can check how the baking is going.

In a smaller bakery, the baker lifts the bread into the oven on trays. The shelves may move so that the bread is cooked evenly.

The bread must be left to cool completely before it is packed, or it will not keep well. In large bakeries, magnets lift the lids from the tins. The bread is sucked out by a machine like a huge vacuum cleaner!

In large bakeries, bread-making is controlled by computer so that mistakes are avoided and hardly any bread is wasted.

The bread travels through a large bakery on conveyor belts. Specially designed machines for every stage mean that people's hands never touch the bread.

After cooling, the bread may be sliced before being wrapped by machine. The bags will already have been printed with details such as the baker's name, the weight of the bread, and the ingredients that were used.

Try this!

Look at some bread wrappings and then design your own. First write down everything you want to show. Is it important that some of the bread can be seen through the wrapping?

How would your wrapping be sealed?

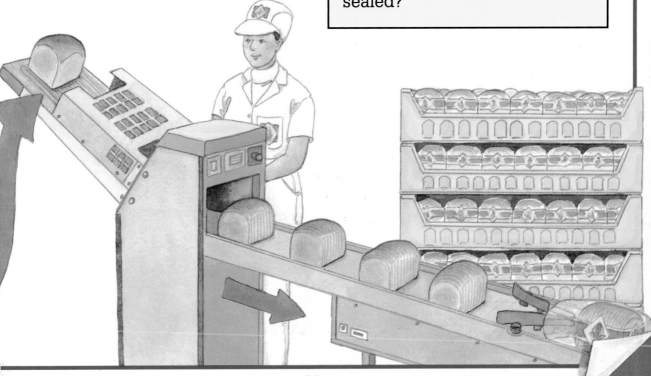

Looking at bread

Different kinds of bread have varying flavours, and uses. They can look different or they may have a certain taste or texture. They may have been made to keep for a long time or a short time. They have different properties which you can find out more about by trying out the tests on these pages.

Record your test results in a scrapbook.

Moist or dry

Fresh bread contains a lot of water. It can quickly become mouldy because the bacteria that make mould need water to grow. Crispbread and bread sticks are drier and will keep longer.

Weigh 60 g of two completely different kinds of bread and leave them in a sunny place for two days. The one that weighs lightest now is the bread that had most water in it.

Shape and size

Draw the shape of the bread in your scrapbook. Why do you think this shape has been chosen? Does this shape of bread have a name?

 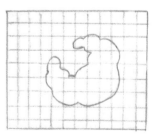

How big is the loaf or roll? You could measure it, or draw round it on squared paper.

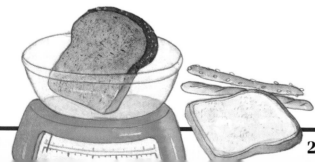

Colour

Make a chart of different colours and number them so that you can use the numbers to describe exactly what colour the bread is. You could use scraps of paper, paints, or even colour charts for house paints to make your scale. Is the inside colour the same as the outside?

Are there little bits of other colours in the bread too? Make a note of them. Can you tell what they are?

Taste and smell

If you are testing how bread tastes, ask an adult to help you check that it is fresh and wash your hands first.

It is hard to describe flavours. Is the bread sweet, salty, nutty, sour? Is it crispy or chewy?

Smell is hard to describe too. Is it yeasty? Floury? No smell at all?

Texture

Can you see lots of little bubbles of air in your bread sample or is it quite solid looking? Some bread has very big air bubbles.

You could try to make a scale to describe this, like the colour scale, or you could make a bread print. Just take a square of bread, press it gently on an ink pad, and then on to paper. With practice you can make a good record of the texture of the bread.

Special breads

Was the bread made for a special occasion, such as Easter or Passover? How is it different from everyday bread?

Make your own bread

This recipe will make three or four small loaves or about 36 rolls. You could make them with some friends and share the kneading and the finished bread. Before you start, make sure your hands and the things you are going to use are very clean.

You will need:

1.5 kg strong plain flour
25 g salt
25 g vegetable fat
25 g fresh yeast
1 teaspoon sugar
900 ml warm water

If you can't find fresh yeast, use dried yeast and follow the instructions on the packet.

1 Mix together the yeast, sugar and 300 ml of the water in a small bowl. Put the mixture in a warm place for 10–15 minutes until it froths.

2 In a large bowl, mix together the flour and salt and rub the fat in with your fingertips.

3 Add the frothy yeast to the flour mixture with the rest of the water and mix it all into a firm dough.

4 Knead the dough for about 5 minutes.

5 Put the dough back in the bowl, cover it and leave it in a warm place to prove until it has doubled in size. Then knead it again.

6 Divide the dough into pieces. Either put these in oiled loaf tins or make them into shapes and put them on oiled baking trays.

Don't fill the tins too full or put rolls too close together.

7 Put the shaped dough in a warm place to prove until it has doubled in size again.

8 You could brush milk or beaten egg on top of the dough before baking.

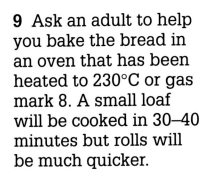

9 Ask an adult to help you bake the bread in an oven that has been heated to 230°C or gas mark 8. A small loaf will be cooked in 30–40 minutes but rolls will be much quicker.

Try this!

You can make your rolls into lots of different shapes before you bake them.

Make letters to spell your name or send a message.

Snip the unbaked roll with scissors to make a hedgehog.

Make three strips of dough and plait them together.

Sprinkle seeds or nuts on top of your rolls.

Watch out!

- Remember that yeast is a living thing. Don't let your dough get too hot or too cold or the yeast may not work.

- Keep everything around you clean and tidy as you make your bread.

Bake-it-yourself

Once you can make bread, you can use the basic recipe to produce all sorts of delicious and fun foods.

Pizza faces

You will need:
bread dough (see pages 22–23)
tomato purée or pasta sauce
cheese
anything you like – peppers, cooked meat or fish, olives, onions, sausage, bacon . . .

1 After you have kneaded the dough twice, make it into circles about 1 cm deep and as big as a small plate. Put them on oiled baking trays.

2 Spread some tomato puree or sauce on the dough and then decorate the pizza faces with other foods. Use these ideas or invent your own!

3 There's no need to let the dough rise again. Just cook your pizzas in a hot oven as before for about 10–15 minutes.

Play bread

You can't eat this dough mixture, but you can make model breads for a dolls' house or model shop.

1 Mix 100 g plain flour, 1 tsp oil, 100 g salt with enough water to make a soft dough.

2 Make small dough models and bake them for 10–20 minutes at 180°C or gas mark 4.

Paint the cooled models with poster paint.

Harvest bread

In some countries a wheatsheaf made of bread is baked after a harvest. Ask friends to help you make one using the recipe on pages 22–23.

1 After kneading the dough twice, take a third of it and make a flat shape to fit a big baking tray.

2 Save a small lump of dough and with the rest make wheat stalks by rolling small pieces of dough into long thin shapes.

3 Make slightly fatter sausages of dough and carefully snip one side to look like an ear of wheat.

4 Lay the wheat stalks and ears on the base and keep adding more until you have a sheaf of wheat.

5 Then make two thin sausages and twirl them together like a rope to put across the sheaf.

6 Finally, make a little mouse to nibble at the stalks.

7 Brush some beaten egg carefully over the sheaf and leave it to prove.

8 Bake the bread in a hot oven as before. Ask an adult to help you check when it is ready.

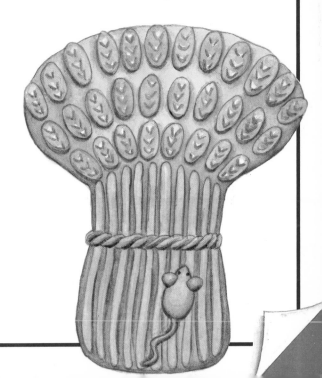

Try this!

If you do not want to eat your sheaf, leave it for a few days and then varnish it. It will keep for a long time like this. You can varnish any kind of bread to make a project display.

Bread past . . .

◆ People have been making some kind of bread for thousands of years. One of the reasons early people had bad teeth was because their bread was full of bits of grit from the stones they used to grind their flour.

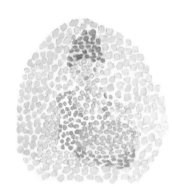

◆ Some bakeries in Roman times were huge. In Rome, more than 25,000 kg of flour were used every day to bake bread for 20,000 people.

◆ In the Middle Ages, flat loaves of bread called trenchers were often used as plates by rich people. When they had finished eating, the trencher might be given to poor people or animals to eat.

◆ In the eighteenth century, bakers added all kinds of things to flour to make their bread whiter. Dried bones, ash, chalk, lime and lead were added. Some of these were poisonous!

◆ Before steam and electrical power were used, mills were powered by wind, water or animals on a treadmill.

... and present

◆ Nowadays sandwiches are a popular way of eating bread all over the world. The story is that they were named after the Earl of Sandwich, who started putting his food between slices of bread so that he didn't have to stop playing cards to have a meal.

◆ In countries such as Canada, where the winters are very cold, farmers use a fast-growing wheat that can be sown and harvested within about 90 days.

◆ A single grain of wheat makes about 20,000 particles of flour.

◆ For hundreds of years only rich people could afford white bread and wholemeal bread was looked down on. Now we know that wholemeal bread is actually more healthy than white bread!

◆ The largest loaf ever baked in a pan weighed 1,435 kilograms. It was 3 metres long and more than a metre high. It was baked in 1988.

Glossary

Bacteria
Tiny kinds of plant that feed on materials and break them down.

Beard
The hairy tufts at the top of each grain in an ear of wheat.

Bran
The outer skin of a wheat grain.

Bread
A food made by moistening, kneading and baking flour.

Cereals
Grasses grown to supply grain for human food.

Dough
Flour mixed with water to make a moist, stretchy mass that is made into bread.

Endosperm
The starchy white centre of a wheat grain.

Fermentation
The process of turning sugar into alcohol and carbon dioxide.

Flour
The seeds of cereals ground down into a fine powder.

Gluten
A protein in flour that makes dough sticky and stretchy.

Grain
The seeds of grasses used for human or animal food.

Gristing
Mixing different kinds of wheat together before milling into flour.

Husk
A leaf-like covering around a single grain of wheat.

Improvers
Ingredients such as ascorbic acid (Vitamin C) added to bread dough to help the yeast work more quickly.

Milling
Grinding grain into flour.

Proving
Letting yeast work in bread dough so that it is filled with bubbles of carbon dioxide to make it rise.

Semolina
Particles of wheat endosperm before it is crushed into flour.

Straw
The stalks and leaves of grain left when the seed heads have been removed.

Strong flour
Flour containing a large amount of gluten.

Wheatgerm
The part of a wheat grain from which a new plant could grow.

White flour
Flour made using only the endosperm of the grain.

Wholemeal flour
Flour made using all parts of the grain.

Yeast
A kind of fungus that digests sugar to form alcohol and carbon dioxide gas.

Index